W9-ATY-399

CREATE with
DUCT
TAPE

DUCT TAPE
Costumes

by Carolyn Bernhardt

Lerner Publications • Minneapolis

Lerner Publications Company
A division of Lerner Publishing Group, Inc.
241 First Avenue North
Minneapolis, MN 55401 USA

For reading levels and more information, look up this title at www.lernerbooks.com.

Main body text set in Bembo. Typeface provided by Monotype.

Library of Congress Cataloging-in-Publication Data

Names: Bernhardt, Carolyn, author.
Title: Duct tape costumes / by Carolyn Bernhardt.
Description: Minneapolis : Lerner Publications, [2016] | Series: Create with duct tape | Audience: Ages 7-11. | Audience: Grades 4 to 6. | Includes bibliographical references and index.
Identifiers: LCCN 2016018666 (print) | LCCN 2016020249 (ebook) | ISBN 9781512426670 (lb : alk. paper) | ISBN 9781512427646 (eb pdf)
Subjects: LCSH: Tape craft--Juvenile literature. | Duct tape--Juvenile literature. | Costume--Juvenile literature. | Handicraft--Juvenile literature.
Classification: LCC TT869.7 .B46924 2016 (print) | LCC TT869.7 (ebook) | DDC 745.59--dc23

LC record available at https://lccn.loc.gov/2016018666

Manufactured in the United States of America
1-41433-23338-8/10/2016

Contents

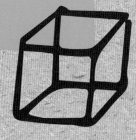

Super Tape

What is tough enough to bind metal but thin and easy to fold? It's soft like cloth. It's surprisingly strong. It's super sticky. It's duct tape!

This cloth-like tape was first known as duck tape. This was because it is **waterproof**, similar to a duck's feathers. Duck tape was originally used by soldiers. They used it to patch military vehicles during World War II (1939–1945). The tape was tough and stuck very well. Word of this trusty tape soon spread. People began using it for all types of tasks, such as connecting **air ducts**. This use became so common that the tape became known as duct tape.

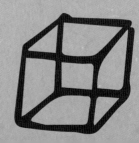

Duct tape has since been used for much more than repairing. People create all kinds of things with it. Many even wear it! Duct tape makes it easy to craft cool costumes and **accessories**, no sewing needed. Imagine making bright dinosaur spikes, colorful alien antennae, and tremendously tough superhero accessories. Then grab a roll and get ready to create duct tape costumes!

Strong Strings

Duct tape's strength comes from its special fibers. These fibers are woven into the tape in a crisscross pattern. They keep duct tape secure under lots of pressure.

Before You
Get Started

Sticky Supply

Duct tape's super stickiness is great for creating entire outfits without a needle and thread. You won't need zippers or buttons either. Any additional accessories can be purchased at craft stores or found online. You can connect pieces, make straps, and more just by sticking duct tape strips together. But the amazing stickiness of this tape can also be a challenge. Strips can easily stick together when you don't want them to, making them hard to separate. So work slowly and carefully as you create your costumes. This will help you avoid wasting tape or sticking the wrong pieces together.

Setting Up a Workspace

It's important to create a clean workspace before beginning your costume crafts. Make sure you have a clear area to work. You don't want your tape to stick to **delicate** surfaces or pick up bits of trash. Place any tools and supplies in easy reach. And keep track of any small parts in bowls or containers. Be aware that duct tape can be difficult to remove from certain surfaces. It may leave a gummy **residue** behind. Check with an adult first before placing tape on your work table. Also make sure any items that will be covered in duct tape are okay to use.

Creative Costume Making

Making costumes is all about creativity! A costume can be as wild or wacky as you want. It can have any awesome accessories or gadgets you can imagine. The possibilities are endless! Duct tape is perfect for making anything you dream up easy to create. Stick flat strips together at their edges to make duct tape sheets. Fold long strips into ties or strings. Wad several strips into balls to make sculptural shapes. What other shapes or forms can you create with duct tape? Think about it and try it out! Use your imagination. Then get busy making creative costumes that feature your own unique additions!

Stay Safe

It's important to stay safe when using and wearing duct tape items. Never press duct tape's sticky side directly to skin. Do not place duct tape on your or someone else's face. Never place it over eyes, ears, or mouths. And never bind any body part with duct tape. Finally, be careful when using sharp objects, such as scissors. Always check in with an adult before working on the crafts in this book.

Custom
Crown

Decorate a fancy duct tape crown fit for royalty!

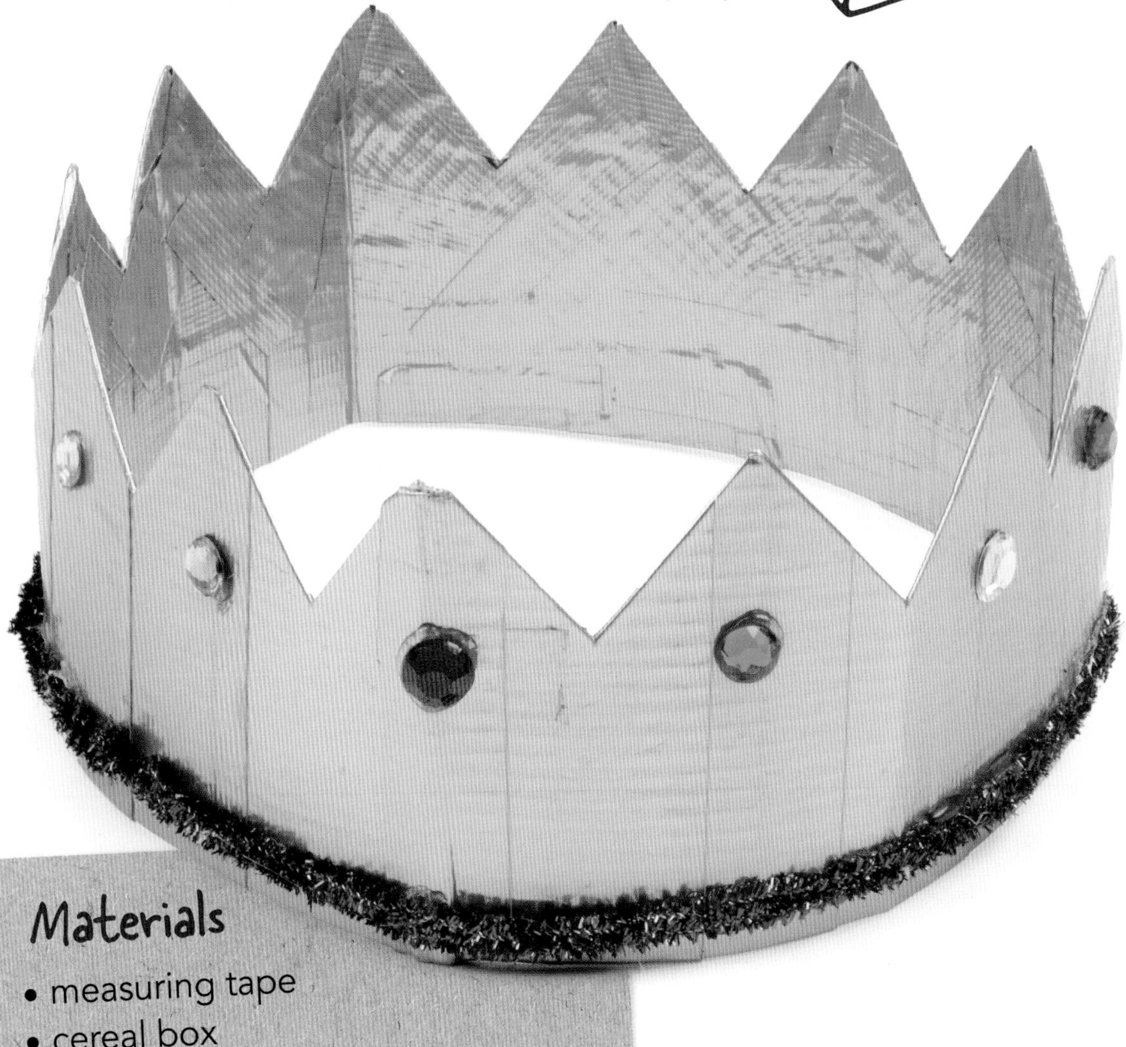

Materials

- measuring tape
- cereal box
- scissors
- ruler
- marker
- duct tape
- optional: gems, craft foam, paint, pipe cleaners

1. Measure around your head with the measuring tape.

2. Take the cereal box apart. Cut the cardboard in half the long way, making two strips. Tape the short edge of one strip to the short edge of the other strip.

3. Use a ruler to draw a flat crown shape onto the cardboard. It should be as long as your head measurement. Cut out the crown.

4. Cover the crown in duct tape. Wrap tape around the sharp points. Cover the back too.

5. Get creative with different shapes, colors, and patterns to decorate the crown. You can even use gems, craft foam, or paint.

6. Tape the crown into a circular shape that fits your head comfortably. Then rule your kingdom in your regal new crown!

3

4

5

Ancient Soldier Shield

Ready yourself for battle with this sturdy shield!

Materials

- marker
- cardboard
- scissors
- duct tape
- optional: brass **brads**, craft foam, gems, glue, paint, paintbrushes

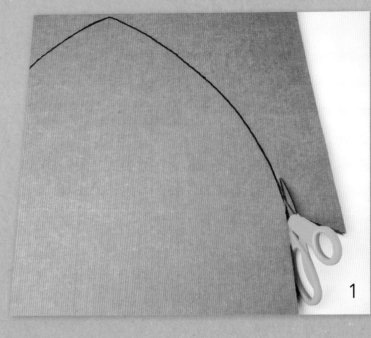

1 Draw a large shield on the cardboard. Cut it out.

2 Cut two strips of duct tape long enough to wrap around your **forearm** once. Lay one on top of the other, pressing the sticky sides together. Repeat for a second strap. These will be your shield's handles.

3 Tape the handles to the back of the shield. Secure them with extra tape to keep them sturdy.

4 Cover the shield with duct tape. Decorate the shield. Attach brass brads to the front for a shiny, metallic look. Add bright gems, or paint an imaginary **crest**. Escape sticky situations with your new duct tape shield!

Did You Know?

Each year, the nonprofit organization Destination Imagination holds a Duct Tape Costume Ball.

Awesome
Animal
Ears

Dress your head in an amazing pair of animal ears!

Materials

- headband
- duct tape
- marker
- cardboard
- scissors

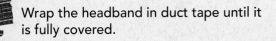
Wrap the headband in duct tape until it is fully covered.

Draw animal ears on the cardboard. They can look like whatever animal's ears you'd like. Cut out the ears.

Cut two strips of duct tape. They should be long enough to wrap around the headband. Attach the short end of one strip to the bottom of one ear. Pull the strip's tail under the headband to attach to the opposite side of the ear. This should secure the ear in place. Repeat this step for the other ear.

Cover the ears with duct tape. Use any pattern or color you want. Wear your awesome new ears and transform into a roaring, wild animal!

Duct Tape
Top Hat

Construct a dashing tape top hat that makes a classy costume all on its own!

Materials
- plastic container
- marker
- cardboard
- measuring tape
- scissors
- duct tape
- optional: craft feathers, gems, paint

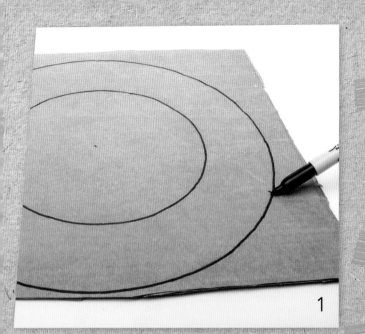

1. Select a container. It should be able to rest comfortably on your head without falling over your eyes. Trace the container's opening on the cardboard. Then, draw a larger circle around the first. There should be about 2 inches (5 centimeters) between the circles.

2. Cut along both circles to create a ring. This will be the hat's **brim**. Cover it in duct tape.

3. Cover the outside of the plastic container with duct tape.

4. Tape the container to the hat's brim until it is secure.

5. Create awesome additions to give your top hat a theme! Stick on bold duct tape stripes, attach a bright feather, and more.

6. Wear your dashing hat to transform any old outfit into a classy costume!

Did You Know?

The largest gathering of people wearing duct tape took place in Knoxville, Tennessee. There, 752 people rocked duct tape costumes!

Duct Tape
Dinosaur

Dress up like a dandy duct tape dinosaur!

Materials

- measuring tape
- duct tape
- scissors
- marker
- cardboard

1 Measure around your head with the measuring tape. Cut a strip of duct tape as long as the measurement. Then fold it in half the long way, pressing the sticky sides together. Tape the strip into a loop. This will be the hat's base.

2 Cut two strips of duct tape about 4 feet (1.2 meters) long. Lay one strip on top of the other, pressing the sticky sides together. This will be your dino spine. Tape the short end of the spine to the hat's base.

3

3 Place the base on your head with the spine in front. Pull the spine over the top of your head, toward your back. Ask an adult to mark where the spine touches the base. Remove the headpiece. Tape the spine to the marked section of the base. When worn, it should trail down your back toward the floor.

4

4 Cut twelve strips of tape 10 inches (25.4 cm) long. Starting at the base, stick one strip against the underside of the spine. Pinch the strip, pressing the sticky sides together, so it is folded around the spine. Repeat all the way down the spine. Then trim the strips into triangle shapes to look like spikes.

5 Draw dinosaur feet on the cardboard. Draw a circle in the center of each foot. Make sure the circles are large enough to slip your feet through. Cut the feet out. Then cut the center holes out.

6 Cover your dinosaur feet in duct tape so they match your headpiece. But be sure to leave the holes uncovered. Slip your feet through the holes. The dinosaur feet should sit on top of your shoes. Put on the headpiece and roam around roaring like your favorite dinosaur!

6

Sidekick
on a Stick

Create a steed sidekick you
can actually ride!

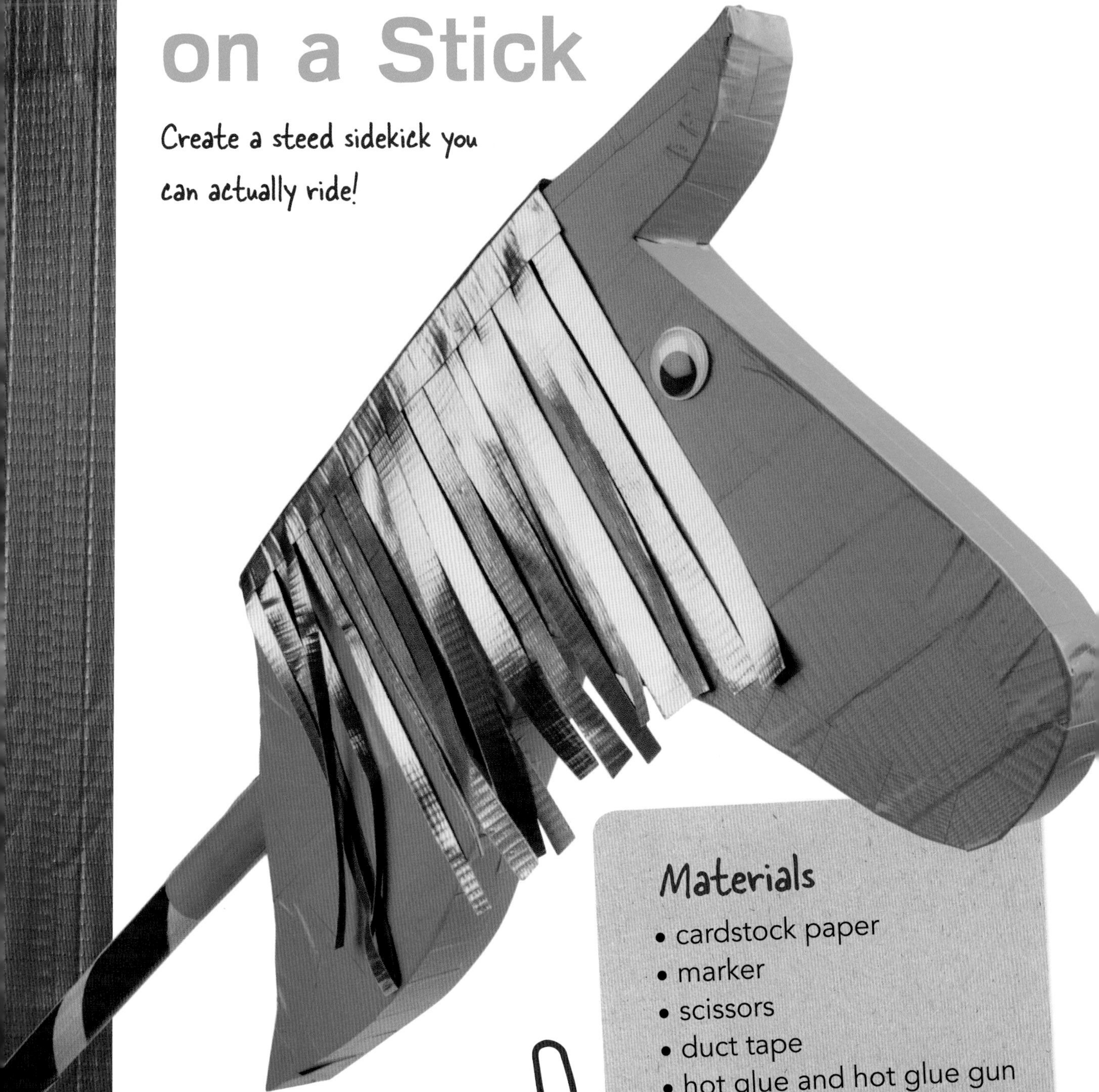

Materials

- cardstock paper
- marker
- scissors
- duct tape
- hot glue and hot glue gun
- googly eyes
- broomstick

Draw a horse, dragon, or other animal head on the cardstock paper. The drawing should be a side view of the animal's head. Cut it out. Trace it and cut out another one.

Cover the cutouts in duct tape. Then cut a strip of cardstock paper as long as their border. Tape the cutouts together, securing the strip in between them. Leave the bottom of the neck open.

If your sidekick needs a mane, cut two long strips of duct tape. Lay one strip on top of the other, pressing the sticky sides together. Cut this long strip into shorter thin strips. These will form the mane.

Cut two long strips of tape. Lay one strip sticky-side up. Attach the mane strips along one edge. Sandwich these with the other long strip, pressing the sticky sides together. Tape the mane to the neck.

With an adult's help, hot glue the googly eyes onto your sidekick.

Tape the head to the top of a broomstick. Then ride your trusty duct tape sidekick across the land!

Amazing
Alien
Antennae

Get galactic with an alien hat that's out of this world!

Materials

- paper or plastic bowl
- duct tape
- pushpin
- stretchy string
- scissors
- 2 bendy straws
- 2 foam balls
- hot glue and hot glue gun
- googly eyes

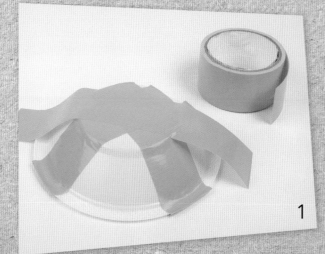

1 Cover the bowl in duct tape.

2 Use the pushpin to poke a small hole in each side of the bowl. Thread the string through the holes, tying a knot at each end. Secure the knots with duct tape.

3 Stick each bendy straw into a foam ball. These will be the antennae. Cover them in duct tape.

4 Use the scissors to cut two X-shapes into the top of the bowl. Poke the straws through the holes. Secure the straws with tape, both on the inside and the outside of the bowl.

5 With an adult's help, hot glue googly eyes onto the antennae. Then blast off to new planets wearing your cosmic cap. Use your awesome eyeball antennae to blend in with the aliens!

Did You Know?
The amount of duct tape sold each year could stretch to the moon and back!

Wearable Wings

Let these neat, no-tear wings take you on an imaginary, high-flying adventure!

Sizing Your Straps

After you attach the wing straps, try them on. If they're too large, carefully remove and trim one end of each strap. Reattach them to the wings and try them on again.

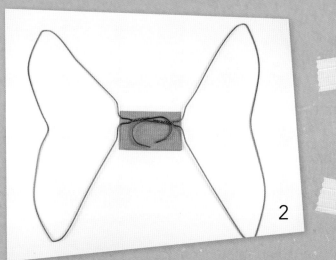

2

1 Pull the bottom of each hanger downward. This will bend the hangers into a diamond shape. Then press the center bends inward to make each hanger look like a wing.

2 Cut two rectangular pieces of cardboard about 3.5 by 4.25 inches (8.9 x 10.8 cm). Sandwich the hooks between the cardboard rectangles. Secure them with tape.

3 Completely cover both wings with tape.

4 Decorate the wings however you want! You can deck them out with felt, duct tape shapes, craft foam, or construction paper.

5 Cut a strip of tape long enough to be a comfortable backpack strap. Then cut a slightly longer strip. Lay one strip on top of the other, pressing the sticky sides together. The longer strip should have some of its sticky side exposed on each end. Make a second strap the same way.

6 Use the sticky ends to attach your straps to the back of your wings. Then imagine you are flying through the skies on your supercool wings!

Super Suit

Save the day, the city, or even the universe in this daring duct tape suit!

Materials

- scissors
- plastic tablecloth
- string
- duct tape
- paper towel tube
- paper
- marker
- pushpin
- stretchy string

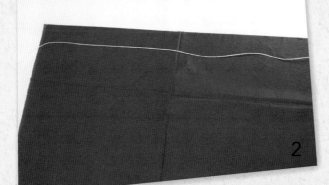

Sticky Tip

Create your own character!
You could be anything from
a lightning-throwing alien to a
superstrong muscle marvel. It's
totally up to you!

Cape

 Cut the tablecloth into the shape you want for your cape.

 Lay a piece of string 1 inch (2.5 cm) below the top edge of the cape. Fold the top edge down over the string. Tape in place.

 Decorate your cape with duct tape. Make your own superhero emblem. Or cover the whole thing in tape.

Arm Cuffs

Cut the paper towel tube in half. Cut a slit along the side of each half.

Cover your cuffs in tape. Then decorate them to match your cape!

Super Suit continued next page

Mask

Draw a mask on a piece of paper. Cut it out. Hold it against your face to make sure it fits properly.

Cut three strips of duct tape as wide as you want your mask to be. Overlap the long edge of one strip slightly with the long edge of another strip. Keep them sticky-side up. Repeat with the remaining strip. Cover this rectangle with more duct tape strips, pressing the sticky sides together. Trace the paper mask onto this duct tape sheet.

Cut the mask out. Use the pushpin to make a hole in each side of the mask.

Measure and cut the stretchy string so that it rests comfortably around your face. Then thread string through each hole. Adjust the fit if necessary Tie a knot on each side and cover it with duct tape.

Decorate your mask to match the arm bands and the cape. Then put on your duct tape suit and go save the world!

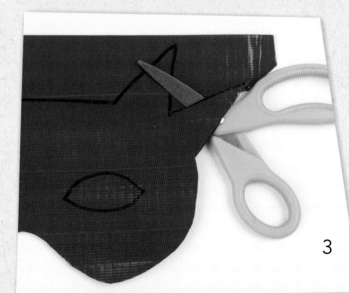

Perform in Your
Awesome Costumes!

Now that you have filled your wardrobe with some clever creations, it's time to pull it all together! Use that same sparkling imagination to create a dramatic play. Or, travel to far off places in your own movie! Write a script, cast the characters, and record it with a camera. Which costume should your main character wear? Which costumes really set the scene? Two minds are better than one, so make sure to include a friend in your production process.

Cleanup and Safekeeping

Now that you've turned this tough tape into creative costumes, it's time to clean up. Pick up all tools and supplies. Throw away any ruined strips, or save them for later costumes. Store duct tape rolls out of the sun.

To keep your duct tape costumes in good shape, store them out of the sun or direct heat. If the tape gets too hot, its glue can become gummy. If any of your items become broken from wear, patch and repair them with more tape.

Keep Creating!

Duct tape can be used to make supercool costumes. But the outfits and accessories you created are just the beginning. Get inspired by the duct tape items you made. Think about what additions or additional costumes you could create. Then, gather more tape and keep crafting!

Glossary

accessories: small items that you wear with your clothes

air ducts: pipes that move air around buildings

brads: slender wire nails with small barrel-shaped heads

brim: the edge of a hat that sticks out over the face of the person wearing it

crest: a symbol or design used to represent a family, group, or organization

delicate: finely made or sensitive

forearm: the part of the arm between the elbow and the wrist

residue: what remains after something else is removed or completed

waterproof: designed to prevent water from entering

Further Information

Davis, Forest Walker. *Duct Tape: 101 Adventurous Ideas for Art, Jewelry, Flowers, Wallets, and More.*
Beverly, MA: Quarry Books, 2015.
Practice your duct tape skills with activities written by a master duct tape artist.

How Duck Tape® Was Named
http://duckbrand.com/about
Learn the history behind one of the most famous duct tape brands.

Morgan, Richela Fabian. *Tape It & Make It: 101 Duct Tape Activities.*
Hauppauge, NY: Barron's, 2012.
Make everything from wallets to flowers to sneaky disguises with this duct tape craft book.

Victoria and Albert Museum: Costume
http://www.vam.ac.uk/page/c/costume/
London's Victoria and Albert museum displays more than 3,500 costume pieces. Take a sneak peek into this famous collection!

Index

Photo Acknowledgments

The images in this book are used with the permission of: © kate_sept2004/iStockphoto, p. 22 (boy); © Lorraine Boogich/iStockphoto, p. 9; © mama_mia/Shutterstock Images, pp. 3, 10, 11, 12, 14, 16, 17, 18, 20, 22, 29, 23, 24, 26, 30; © monkeybusinessimages/iStockphoto, p. 7; © Mighty Media, Inc., pp. 1 (yellow tape), 4 (glitter tape), 5 (hat craft), 5 (teal tape), 5 (yellow tape), 6 (teal tape), 7 (glitter tape), 8 (superhero craft), 8 (teal tape), 8 (yellow tape), 9 (yellow tape), 10 (teal tape), 11 (teal tabs), 11 (top), 11 (middle), 11 (bottom), 12 (yellow tape), 13 (top), 13 (middle), 13 (bottom), 13 (yellow tabs), 13 (yellow tape), 14 (ears craft), 15 (top), 15 (middle), 15 (bottom), 15 (red tab), 16 (hat craft), 16 (teal tape), 17 (top), 17 (middle), 17 (bottom), 17 (yellow tape), 18 (wings craft), 18 (yellow tape), 19 (top), 19 (middle), 19 (bottom), 20 (sidekick craft), 21 (red tab), 21 (top), 21 (middle), 21 (bottom), 22 (alien craft), 22 (teal tape), 23 (teal tabs), 23 (yellow tape), 23 (top), 23 (middle), 23 (bottom), 24 (dino feet), 24 (yellow tape), 25 (top), 25 (middle), 25 (bottom), 25 (yellow tabs), 26 (superhero craft), 27 (red tab), 27 (top), 27 (middle), 27 (bottom), 28 (top), 28 (middle), 28 (bottom), 29 (purple tape), 29 (glitter tape), 29 (yellow tape), 30 (glitter tape), 31 (yellow tape), 32 (yellow tape), 32 (green tape); © Syda Productions/Shutterstock Images, p. 29 (boy); © wongwean/Shutterstock Images, pp. 4, 6 (yellow paper), 13 (green paper), 15 (yellow paper), 19 (green paper), 21 (yellow paper), 25 (green paper), 27 (yellow paper), 28 (yellow paper), 30 (green paper).

Cover: © Feng Yu/Shutterstock Images (gray tape roll); © Mighty Media, Inc.; © wongwean/Shutterstock Images (green background).

Back Cover: © Feng Yu/Shutterstock Images (gray tape roll); © wongwean/Shutterstock Images (green background).